# a pocketful of
# RHYME
*Imagination for a new generation*

2006 Poetry Competition for 7-11 year-olds

YoungWriters

# Lancashire Vol II
Edited by Carrie Ghazanfer

 Young**Writers**

First published in Great Britain in 2006 by:
Young Writers
Remus House
Coltsfoot Drive
Peterborough
PE2 9JX
Telephone: 01733 890066
Website: www.youngwriters.co.uk

SB ISBN 1 84602 614 8

# Foreword

Young Writers was established in 1991 and has been passionately devoted to the promotion of reading and writing in children and young adults ever since. The quest continues today. Young Writers remains as committed to the nurturing of poetic and literary talent as ever.

This year's Young Writers competition has proven as vibrant and dynamic as ever and we are delighted to present a showcase of the best poetry from across the UK and in some cases overseas. Each poem has been selected from a wealth of A Pocketful Of Rhyme entries before ultimately being published in this, our fourteenth primary school poetry series.

Once again, we have been supremely impressed by the overall quality of the entries we have received. The imagination, energy and creativity which has gone into each young writer's entry made choosing the poems a challenging and often difficult but ultimately hugely rewarding task - the general high standard of the work submitted ensured this opportunity to bring their poetry to a larger appreciative audience.

We sincerely hope you are pleased with this final collection and that you will enjoy A Pocketful Of Rhyme Lancashire Vol II for many years to come.

# Contents

## Coppull Parish Church School

| | |
|---|---|
| Laura Blow  (9) | 33 |
| Jack Cutts  (9) | 34 |
| Pashé Taylor  (9) | 35 |
| Kate Brennan  (10) | 36 |
| Reece Barrow  (10) | 37 |
| Chloe Bennett  (9) | 38 |
| Lauren Conway  (10) | 39 |
| Sandy Hayes  (10) | 40 |
| Jessica Bennett  (10) | 41 |
| Daniel Jeffrey  (10) | 42 |
| Campbell Fryer  (10) | 43 |
| Jessica Halstead  (10) | 44 |
| Paige Howarth  (9) | 45 |
| Chelsea Wilkinson  (10) | 46 |
| Amy Nice  (10) | 47 |
| Ryan Ashcroft  (10) | 48 |
| Rebecca Robinson  (10) | 49 |
| Jack Ashworth  (10) | 50 |

## Cuerden Church School

| | |
|---|---|
| Ryan Davies  (10) | 51 |
| Bethany Holt  (9) | 52 |
| Shannon Smith  (10) | 53 |
| Jack Turner  (10) | 54 |
| Jayne Monks  (10) | 55 |
| Dawn Ditchfield  (10) | 56 |
| Amy Robertson  (9) | 57 |
| Ann Scrivens  (10) | 58 |
| Jodi Moore  (10) | 59 |
| Naomi Evans  (10) | 60 |
| Dani Moore  (10) | 61 |
| Alice Bridges  (10) | 62 |
| Danielle Kay  (8) | 63 |
| Mellisa Allonby  (9) | 64 |
| Lauren Smith  (8) | 65 |
| Georgia Madden  (9) | 66 |
| Natasha Kuerschner  (8) | 67 |
| Jack Carr  (9) | 68 |
| Aaron Holland  (9) | 69 |
| Callum Leithes  (8) | 70 |

| Ben Duckworth (8) | 71 |
|---|---|
| Alex Ashworth (7) | 72 |
| Jake Holt (7) | 73 |
| Reece Thomas (8) | 74 |
| Chelsea Porter (8) | 75 |
| Tyler Walmsley (8) | 76 |
| Rhianna Thomas (8) | 77 |
| Billy Scanlon (7) | 78 |
| Shannon Scanlon (7) | 79 |
| Dominic Walmsley (7) | 80 |
| Matthew Jones (8) | 81 |

## Garstang Community Primary School

| Emily Helm (11) | 82 |
|---|---|
| William Yates (11) | 83 |
| Anna Crowther (10) | 84 |
| Amy Winder (11) | 85 |
| Adam Baldwin (11) | 86 |
| Jonathon Thompson (11) | 87 |
| Adam Stone (10) | 88 |
| Laura Sullivan (11) | 89 |
| Emilie Bickerstaff (11) | 90 |
| Shannon Knape (11) | 91 |
| Sam Briault (11) | 92 |
| Katrina Symons (10) | 93 |
| Sophie Greenwood (11) | 94 |
| Jessica Ford (11) | 95 |
| James Gibbins (11) | 96 |
| Shane Taylor (10) | 97 |
| Alistair Swarbrick (10) | 98 |
| Jessica Preston (10) | 99 |
| Helen Winstanley (11) | 100 |
| Joshua Crouch, Curtis Rogers & Lewis Bingham (11) | 101 |
| Alex Dodd (10) | 102 |
| Jack Farrar (11) | 103 |
| Lauren Kemp (11) | 104 |

## Lord Street Primary School

| Yolanda Holden (10) | 105 |
|---|---|
| Jak Manser (11) | 106 |
| Jade Phair (11) | 107 |

Holly Steele-Robinson  (11)                     108
Jordan Brown  (10)                              109
Lauren Ann Goodship  (11)                       110
Aimee Randle  (11)                              111
Sophie Regan  (11)                              112
Andrew Storey  (10)                             113
Luke Ormerod  (10)                              114
Harriet-Faye Webber  (11)                       115
Louise Townson  (11)                            116
Adam Cockcroft  (11)                            117
Nathan McKenzie  (11)                           118
Samantha Sears  (11)                            119
Billy Fryer  (11)                               120
Curtis Davies  (10)                             121

## Norbreck Primary School
Charlotte Whittaker  (11)                       122
Robert Lee  (11)                                123
Frankie Fratazzi  (11)                          124
Rebecca Feay  (11)                              125
Kieran Sefton  (11)                             126
Jordan Butterworth  (11)                        127
Michaela Jacobs  (10)                           128
Gina Fratazzi  (11)                             129
Miri Jones  (10)                                130
Rebecca Nolan  (11)                             131
Jennie McGill  (10)                             132
Chloe Biddlestone  (11)                         133
Libby Matthews  (10)                            134
Ellie Reilly  (11)                              135
Laura White  (11)                               136
Taylor Mitchell  (11)                           137
Chris Davis  (11)                               138
Matthew Lightfoot  (10)                         139
Rebecca Page  (11)                              140
Alex Radcliffe  (10)                            141
Joshua Bailey  (11)                             142
Philip Sayers  (10)                             143
Rebekka Foy  (11)                               144
Kelly Hammersley  (11)                          145
Ashley Crooper Calland  (11)                    146

## Roseacre CP School

| | |
|---|---|
| Lauren Atha  (7) | 147 |
| Laura Anthony  (11) | 148 |
| Gabriella Ann Maud Berry  (11) | 149 |
| Laura Coleman  (7) | 150 |
| Alice Croft  (11) | 151 |
| Shannon Cuthbert  (10) | 152 |
| Christopher Dix  (11) | 153 |
| Donald Hakandu  (11) | 154 |
| Reece Hendry  (11) | 155 |
| Hope Hollis  (10) | 156 |
| Bethany Hunt  (10) | 157 |
| Alexandra Isaac  (10) | 158 |
| Nathan Jackson  (11) | 159 |
| Amanda Johnson  (11) | 160 |
| Jack Lavelle  (11) | 161 |
| Jordan Jessica McLellan  (10) | 162 |
| Sam McCloy  (11) | 163 |
| Jordan Payne  (11) | 164 |
| Jasmine-Lea Senior  (10) | 165 |
| Shashin Sood  (7) | 166 |
| Henry Woodsford  (11) | 167 |

## St Hugh's CE Primary School, Oldham

| | |
|---|---|
| Leon Baker  (7) | 168 |
| Chelsea Dawson  (9) | 169 |
| Georgia Maltby  (9) | 170 |
| Alex Lamb  (11) | 171 |
| Rosie Sutton  (8) | 172 |

## St James' CE Primary School, Haslingden

| | |
|---|---|
| Shurayh Shuaib  (8) | 173 |
| Hafsah Begum  (8) | 174 |
| Ruksana Akter  (8) | 175 |
| Fahmedah Ridwana  (8) | 176 |
| Darius Barton  (7) | 177 |
| Thahmid Hoque  (8) | 178 |
| Tyler Jacques  (8) | 179 |
| Hayley Morley  (11) | 180 |
| Naomi Mandeena  (11) | 181 |
| Jordan Jacques  (10) | 182 |

# The Poems

# Late For School

Wake up in the morning at seven o'clock
Mum shouts, 'Roxie, get up on the dot!
Quick! Quick! Get dressed,
Brush your hair - it looks like a bird's nest!'

Rush! Dash!
Dash! Rush!
Clean my teeth
Hair to brush
School! Dash!
Dash! School!
Got to be early
It's a golden rule!

Eat my breakfast, drink my drink
Put my dishes in the sink
Get the house keys, lock the door
Into the car and dash no more!

**Roxzanna Loftus  (9)**

# My Fantasy

It's a place I go to
Filled with wonder and mystery
It's a place I like to call
My fantasy.

Sweets galore
They're all free,
I eat them all day
In my fantasy.

School is banned
So I can watch TV,
I watch all my programmes
In my fantasy.

Amazing creatures
From the blorg to the yankee,
Big or small, fat or thin
In my fantasy.

Environmentally friendly
As far as the eye can see,
No cities around
In my fantasy.

Evil is banished
There's good in you and me,
No cruelness, only kindness
In my fantasy.

So come to this world
And be friends with me,
We'll have some fun
In my fantasy.

But alas, it's a dream
A shame, it's so lovely,
Until I daydream again
Say goodbye to my fantasy.

**Rebecca Ferguson (10)**
**Arkholme CE School**

# Monkeys

Monkeys decide to stop on trees
Habitats of fruit and leaves
Dancing in rhythm
Howling in happiness
On the move between the branches
Sliding on trees like Tarzan
Packing ripe bananas for hibernation
Swinging in their own insane world.

M aking noises that deafen
O n the trees they remain safe from predators
N o monkeys leave the tribe
K indly sharing bananas
E merging bananas from their skins
Y awning before a good night's sleep
S winging sweetly

But whoa, it spells monkeys!

**Hassan Khan (9)**
**Bolton Parish Church CE School**

# The Sea's Waves

Gigantic waves crashing down
And meeting sand on the ground,
Waves going up and down
The waves getting bigger to touch the sky
And then struggling to get back down.

**Joshua Newbould (10)**
**Bolton Parish Church CE School**

# The Sea's Waves

The sea was clashing against the banks.
The waves softly pushing in and out.
The taste was like salty water,
Like you have never tasted it before.
It smelt like a rotten apple on top of the sea.
The colourful fish, struggling to get in the water.
I could hear the waves going *shhh* into my ears.
I could feel the water which tickles on top of my fingertips.

**Akhil Patel  (9)**
**Bolton Parish Church CE School**

# A Change Of Waves

Following the sun, as it reluctantly sets behind the horizon
A peaceful voyage is travelling through the waves.
There is no wonder or madness,
No clashing or badness,
But that's just the first day.

At night, beyond the pier, the moon is bright,
And a ripple has been made by one sad tear.
Stars shine with love
On the rail is a perched dove.
And that's how the night will go on.

Thunder is feeling in a bad mood,
It throws down a bolt and transforms a wave,
There is fear and no joy
No help and no sailing buoy
This is how bad it can get.

**Alysha Parkinson  (10)**
**Bolton Parish Church CE School**

# The Sensational Sea

The waves were chaotic,
They crashed rapidly against the banks,
They were intimidating the fish
As they struggled to swim over the wild sea.

The cliffs collided with the insane ocean
And the water toppled over the sandy beach,
The tide crashed against the bay
I didn't know what to say.

The shimmering, glimmering sea
Was shivering up and down,
With an almighty frown
There was a deafening sound.

**Kieran Aldred (10)**
**Bolton Parish Church CE School**

# The Sea

The sea bashes onto the pier
Two big dolphins jumping together
The wind is calm and is pretending it is not here
People are diving on top of each other
The sea is a chaotic river
Fish struggling to come out of the river
People having an exotic day
People bring pets like it's always the same.

**Yasin Ali  (9)**
**Bolton Parish Church CE School**

# Waves

W aves clashing together like two cars in a collision
A quamarine fish, splashing and splashing in the waves
'V anish, there goes my ice cream it's that hot,' said Mum
E xcellent dolphins diving up and down in the waves
S oftly the waves quiver back and forth.

**Ruby Ottewill  (10)**
**Bolton Parish Church CE School**

# The Sea

The amazing sea
Expands like a
Huge snake.
The sea rapidly
Forms loops in
The middle of
The ocean.
Two waves crashed
Into each other
Like a mad car
*Crash!*

The wild sea
Toppled onto the
Smooth sand.
The colossal
Waves hit the
Ground like
An earthquake
Shaking the universe.

**Morgan Morton (9)**
**Bolton Parish Church CE School**

# The Wonderful Sea

I see fish jumping up and down.
The sea looks like it is angry.
It smells like acid.
I hear the waves like thunder.
It feels smooth when you touch it.
The water tastes disgusting.
I hear the waves clambering back and forwards.

**Joseph Farrow  (10)**
**Bolton Parish Church CE School**

# The Tidal Wave

Dolphins pounding
While I'm frowning.
A ship hovering across the sea
Just like a bee.

My nose exploding
With the fishy smell.
Lips taste salty
From the sea's spray.

The waves crunching the sand
Like a giant, eating crisps.
The wind combing my hair forwards
And jumping in wisps.

The wind is cold and gritty
People surfing like a leaf dancing on water.
The sun is rising
Like a big golden balloon.

**Joshua Bentley  (10)**
**Bolton Parish Church CE School**

# Tsunami

The sea was clobbering
The banks were falling
The cliffs were colliding with the sea
The tides chaotically crashing

It was streaming and exploding constantly
The waves were like the rampaging tsunami
Surfers were surfing and children wanted to play
No sense of what was coming today.

**Hamza Khan (10)**
**Bolton Parish Church CE School**

# The Sea

The sea was clashing
The waves were leaping
The waves were gigantic
The waves were getting higher and higher
The waves were calm.

**Aysha Saleem  (9)**
**Bolton Parish Church CE School**

# Wigan Team

Wigan are the best team
They shine out like a bright beam.
They can beat any team
Hear the crowd shout and scream.
When they kick the football
It glides through the sky
To the back of the net,
Every night, in my dream!

**Jack Rigby (10)**
**Bryn St Peter's CE School**

# Alphabet Poem

A is for arrow, B is for ball
C for a cat in a cat stall.

D for dog, E for echo
F for fish who claps at art deco.

G for giraffe, H for hamster
I for iguana who acts like a gangster.

J for jacket, K for king
L for leopard who wears bling-bling.

M for master, N for Nick
O for Odie that likes to lick.

P for Peter, Q for queen
R for Robert who likes to scream.

S for stupid, T for tree
U for umbrella that protects me.

V for van, W for winter
X for X-ray that shows a splinter.

Y for yak and also yacht
Z for zebra who talks a lot.

**Thomas Wilkins  (10)**
**Bryn St Peter's CE School**

# Dogs

I went to the pet shop and to my surprise
There were dogs every different shape and size,
They had . . .
Tabby dogs, shabby dogs,
Wild dogs, mild dogs,
Creeping dogs, sleeping dogs,
Prowling dogs, growling dogs,
City dogs, witty dogs,
Lazy dogs, crazy dogs,
Shy dogs, sly dogs,
White dogs, night dogs,
Dancing dogs, prancing dogs,
Slim dogs, trim dogs,
Lanky dogs, swanky dogs,
Frizzy dogs, dizzy dogs,
Moody dogs, broody dogs,
Lean dogs, mean dogs,
Grey dogs, stray dogs,
Hissing dogs, kissing dogs,
Fair dogs, rare dogs,
Grumpy dogs, lumpy dogs,
Old dogs, bold dogs,
Town dogs, brown dogs,
Alas! I came to the last pen
And in the corner all alone
Was a puppy all skin and bone.
I clapped my hands in glee
That puppy was the one for me!

**Heather Collier (10)**
**Bryn St Peter's CE School**

# In The Picture Of Evil

Rock slides crashing down beside me
Bats flickering through the air
An evil witch using dark chi
Poor prisoners in total despair.

A deranged demon chasing me
Bombs exploding in the ground
Jungle cats being set free
And a skeleton has just been found.

All this has happened on one night
I'm totally scared
I've really, really had a fright
And my mum doesn't even care!

**Christian Waddington  (10)**
**Bryn St Peter's CE School**

# My Birthday

It's my birthday today
No horse of course
But plenty of things just as good.
I skipped happily in the rain to school
They sang 'happy birthday' to me, I felt the fool
Finally another school day was complete
I had a birthday cake with lots of sweets
I invited my friend over for tea
Lots of presents, one, two, three
They never forgot me.
And again, no horse of course
It was my birthday today, although it's nearly over
I did find a four-leaf clover.

**Sophie Tootle  (10)**
**Bryn St Peter's CE School**

# My Cat

I have a cat
She really is quite fat
All she does is sleep all day
She is a lazy cat.
In the garden she likes to lie in the sun
That is her idea of fun.
She likes to watch the birds fly about
But you won't catch her running around
And that is all about my cat.

**Michael Taylor  (10)**
**Bryn St Peter's CE School**

# Ode To Poems

P eople like all sorts of poems
O h! the joy of reading poems
E veryone favours at least one sort of poem
M y poem, your poem, even a famous poet's poem
S o please put this in a poetry book
    because lots of people like it and I hope you do too!

**Matthew Middleton (10)**
**Bryn St Peter's CE School**

# The Football Match

Andy Cole missed a goal
Then he stood on a mole.
Peter Crouch shouted, 'Ouch!'
When the ball made him fall.
Malbranquye was small
Crouch was tall,
Baines was the fastest of them all.
The manager hurt his feet
Then the game was complete.
He hit the goal pole
Then he did a forward roll.
He walked away with a weep
When he suffered a defeat.

**Dean Silcock  (9)**
**Bryn St Peter's CE School**

# Going On Holiday

Going on holiday
Is so much fun
And I enjoy the sun
I run
To get an iced bun.

Going on holiday
You have to pay
Especially when you go to Spain
Sometimes it is a pain
But it never rains!

**Lee Ross (10)**
**Bryn St Peter's CE School**

# Roy's Toys

There once was a boy called Roy
Whose girlfriend's name was Joy.
In his dream he wanted to be kissed
But slowly and sadly he missed
And ended up kissing his toy.
But now he's left his one and only girlfriend forever.

**Connor Seddon  (10)**
**Bryn St Peter's CE School**

# In My Dream

In my dream I am a superhero, flying up in the sky
Or am I a long, tall giraffe whose neck is one-hundred metres high?
In my dream I am a beautiful flower
Or am I a yellow lemon, very sweet and very sour?
In my dream I am a ticking clock
Or am I a sparkling, glistening frock?
In my dream I am a writing pen
Or am I a feathery, clucking hen?
In my dream I am a bouncy ball
Or am I asleep and I am nothing at all?

**Stephanie McKee (10)**
**Bryn St Peter's CE School**

# Summer Holidays

When it is sunny
You normally see a bunny.
Put on your suncream
Why people go and buy an ice cream.
Whilst you're playing with your beach ball
People go shopping in the mall.
Put on your summer cap
Then have a nap.
Love the sun
Whilst you have fun.
Go and play with your mates
Whilst people walk on the beach with their dates.
When you are having fun
Remember that summer has only just begun.
With the bags all packed to go
You chuck away your play dough.
When you start to get a tan
Try to make a paper fan.
So there's a poem about summertime
Did you like my lovely rhyme?

**Rebecca Matthews  (10)**
**Bryn St Peter's CE School**

# I Can't Write A Poem

I can't write a poem
It's impossible to do
It's so hard, so please give me a clue.

My brain is not working
No, my head's really hurting.

It's thumping really hard
I wish it were as easy as writing a simple card.

So I can't write a poem
It's just not the thing for me
I'm better at maths you see.

**Jessica Hutton  (10)**
**Bryn St Peter's CE School**

# At The Back Of My Garden

Morning to night there is a sound,
It makes your ears pound,
It's the horses, giving a neigh,
Nobody knows what they're trying to say,
It's only the horses having a play.

When I look at the horses, I feel happy inside,
So give the horses carrots, then you're kind,
The horses are as giddy as boys,
I get a shock and tingles of joy.

The field is shades of green,
Watch what you say, or the horses get mean,
The field is separated into males
And also into females,
The closest to me is the males,
Don't feed them stuff that's pale.
In summer there's a lovely view
People give a *phew!*
And everyone gives food to the horses.

The field's been there since before WWI, so it's old
Since then it's never been sold
In WWII it was hit by a bomb
By a boy called Tom
And now it slants down.

**Robyn Matthews  (10)**
**Bryn St Peter's CE School**

# Shoes

I went to buy a pair of shoes
Oh there were too many to choose!
Big, small, fat, thin, tall, short, high heels,
Wedges, trainers, sandals, flip flops, slip-on ones,
Velcros, laces, buckles, thongs, printed high heels,
Patent, flats, wooden platforms, clogs and football boots.
I just decided in the end not to bother to follow the trend,
A pair of slippers I would wear
What people thought I didn't care!

**Georgia Haimes  (9)**
**Bryn St Peter's CE School**

# Sky!

Birds in the sky
Flying high
Planes from Easyjet
Zooming past my eyes
*Bang, roar, pop!*
The lightning's coming
*Zap, zap, zap!*
The lightning hits your back.

**Caitlin Alcock  (9)**
**Bryn St Peter's CE School**

# In The Summertime

There are lots of lovely flowers
But there are lots of sun showers.
You have got to hang out in the sun
Because it is lots of fun.
Go in the swimming pool
Or go and canoe.
Go to the park
Or get eaten by a shark.
Have a water fight
Until you drop at night.
The sun makes it light
Until you drop at night.
Do your washing
As well, when it is sloshing.
Go to shows
And you can feel your twinkling nose.
Go to the sea
And something might bite your knee.
Go to the shop until you drop
Why don't you play until it is the end of the day
And your mum will say, 'That's enough play for one day.'
As well, get a tan
Until you hear the ice cream van.
Go to a fair
Never worry about your hair.
Go to a party
Enjoy a Smartie.
It is always dry
And the temperate is always high.

**Kerys Whitfield (10)**
**Bryn St Peter's CE School**

# The Zoo

I like the zoo
You can come too.
In the sun
You can have fun.
Monkeys, giraffes, rhinos too
And all the elephants having a poo.

You can go on a ride
Or play on the slide
Or you can take a break
And sail on a lake.
You can go for a walk
And hear the keepers talk.

You can also dine
With a bottle of wine.
You can have tea
And watch a chimpanzee.
At the end of the day
Your mum will say,
'We'll be on our way.'

**Kate Hart (10)**
**Bryn St Peter's CE School**

# Football

F ootball is fantastic
O n the day of the final I tried my very best
O h! It was great and our team won!
T oday I practised football and it was really, really fun
B en, the goalie, saved all our goals
A nd that was how we won
L iam, our midfielder, fell over loads of times
L ater, after the match, I had a shower and got ready for my tea.

**Laura Blow  (9)**
**Coppull Parish Church School**

# What Am I?

Am I an eagle?
Am I a bird?
Am I a seagull
Or even a bear?

Could I be a human?
Could I be a lad?
Could I be a man
Or even a dad?

Is my name Ryan?
Is my name Jack?
Is my name Stephen
Or even Zack?

**Jack Cutts (9)**
**Coppull Parish Church School**

# Friends

F riends make me smile like I've never smiled before
R ight and left I see the sun coming into my life
I hear the song of a bird when my friends are near me
E very minute I wait for them
N ever once did I leave the spot to find them
D id I see a speck of light?
S uddenly, out of nowhere, my happiness comes back.

**Pashé Taylor  (9)**
**Coppull Parish Church School**

# Rabbit Run

I ate the grass while counting the sheep
Until I fell into a deep, deep sleep
I dreamed of some carrots while I sang
But then I heard a mighty *bang!*

I quickly ran before I was seen
But the prey saw me and was very keen
So I went hopping on and landed in a box
Before the thing saw me, which I call a fox!

**Kate Brennan (10)**
**Coppull Parish Church School**

# PGL

The zip wire was fast and fun
The rifles were excellent
The quads wee speedy
The raft building was scary and super
There was a game called 50-50
It was great on the day
The egg race was great and fun
The kayak was funny, fun and great
The fencing was cool and I loved it.

**Reece Barrow  (10)**
**Coppull Parish Church School**

# Animals

There was a snake called Jake
He went in the garden with a rake
He raked up some leaves under some trees
Then went inside for chips and peas.

There was a monkey called Bob
Who had a little monkey job
He had a wife as a boss
Who often got quite cross.

There was a bird called Harry
Who had a girlfriend called Carrie
They went out one night to have a quick bite
Then they ended up having a big fight.

There was a very little duck
Who wasn't very good with luck
A crocodile came up to me
And said, 'Would you like to be my tea?'

**Chloe Bennett  (9)**
**Coppull Parish Church School**

# Raft Building

R afting is exciting, joyful and amazing
A t least we all stayed on the raft
F or no matter how many times we jumped in, we never fell off
T o our amazement, someone started splashing us

B elly-flops, we all jumped in making lots of noise
U nder the water, paddles were working
I started jumping in the water, making a big splash
L ying flat on the raft was so good and fun
D aring to jump in was so exciting
I saw people rowing and rowing, tiring themselves out
N ear the trees there were rafts flowing past
G oing near to the edge, the journey is over.

**Lauren Conway  (10)**
**Coppull Parish Church School**

# Sunset

Sunset sets down on the moving Earth
Bouncing away from the mottled mountains
Skimming all the rivers
Reflecting the clouds.

Sunsets are perfect pink, baby-blue, ruby-red and others too.
But for some reason, I never know
Where the sun goes when the moon comes through.

**Sandy Hayes (10)**
**Coppull Parish Church School**

# Zip Wire

Z ip wire is thrilling
I n your face, the wind is blowing
P eople waving as you go by

W hen you're zipping through the sky
I t's really exciting
R eally, it's not frightening
E nding at last with a smile on your face.

**Jessica Bennett (10)**
**Coppull Parish Church School**

# A Fencing Rap

You've got to be quick on your feet,
Got to move with the beat.
Got to be aware,
Got to watch and take care.

You've got to move real fast,
Or you won't have a blast.
You've got to joust quite good
From where your feet are stood.

You've got to poke in the chest
So that you'll be the best.
You've got to get some good shots,
You've got to get lots and lots.

**Daniel Jeffrey  (10)**
**Coppull Parish Church School**

# Sounds In School

Sounds in school
Sounds in class
Sounds in the hallway
Sounds are all around
Reception are screaming and shouting out loud
Year 5 are silent and don't make a sound
I went to the office; the secretary was on the phone
The kettle was boiling hot and the tea was splashing in the pot
Everywhere are sounds
They're running all around.

**Campbell Fryer  (10)**
**Coppull Parish Church School**

# Fishy Tale

I am a little fishy called Molly
I don't have much use for a brolly
I swim around in my bowl day after day
But when the cat comes
I swim away!

**Jessica Halstead  (10)**
**Coppull Parish Church School**

# Excitement

Excitement is red like a fireball.
Orange is like red.
It sounds like fire is in your head, burning like mad.
It tastes like a toffee fireball (when you eat it, it is boiling hot like Saturn)
It smells like ruby-red flowers.
It looks like a birthday cake; it's got a golden medal
                                on the sparkling icing.
It feels like boiling hot water.
It reminds me of Saturn.

**Paige Howarth  (9)**
**Coppull Parish Church School**

# The Travellers

The travellers are so strong
Where will they go? Nobody knows.
The travellers are so busy
What will they do now? Nobody knows.
The travellers are waiting
What are they waiting for? Nobody knows.
The mysterious ways of the travellers.

**Chelsea Wilkinson (10)**
**Coppull Parish Church School**

# Waiting

I'm waiting for the duck to set off for food
So I can swoop down and grab on to the only egg.
Sitting on the bramble bush watching her paddle off
                                    into the distance, I wait.
It's starting to get cold, I have to be quick before the duck
                                    returns to keep warm.
*Swoosh!*
I swing down like I'm sat on a swing
*Swoosh!*
I've caught it, now to fly off!

**Amy Nice  (10)**
**Coppull Parish Church School**

# Red Dragons

R oaring, it lurks behind

E dging closer, it attacks its prey

D ragons, dragons, surely the best

D rawing you in

R acing across the sky

A s you get a tingle down your spine

G ripping you until blood pours out of your head

O range blood inside its mind

N ipping in and out of corners

S kimming your very own flesh.

**Ryan Ashcroft (10)**
**Coppull Parish Church School**

# Football Mad

Your heart beats strong
Stronger than it has before
And when the whistle has gone
That is when it starts.
Your feet begin to tackle and the ball starts to glide
Your arms begin to wave.
It's like you're speeding and jumping across, chasing a wild cheetah
And when you score you feel great.
The final whistle has gone, all of this has gone
Your power has gone and everything has disappeared.

**Rebecca Robinson (10)**
**Coppull Parish Church School**

# PGL

Quads were quadtastic
Fencing was fantastic
Air rifles were airtacular
Zip wire was ziptastic
Egg race was eggsotic
Kayaks was kayaktic
Raft building was raftsotic
All of it was the best!

**Jack Ashworth (10)**
**Coppull Parish Church School**

# Wrestle Mania 22

As rough as a brick
The wrestler
As strong as a giant.
Heavy like a car and truck.
Rey Mysterio or Randy Orton
For the World Heavyweight Championship?

John Cena or Triple H
For the WWE Championship?
Kane or the Big Show,
Who will win?

**Ryan Davies (10)**
Cuerden Church School

# In The Kitchen

*Sizzle, sizzle* go the sausages turning golden brown.
*Pop, bang* goes the lid of the pan when you're making vegetables.
*Ping* goes the oven when it's ready with delicious pizza.

**Bethany Holt (9)**
**Cuerden Church School**

# Underwater World

I can see tropical fish darting through the underworld.
The shiny scales shimmer in the sea.
The colours of the fish are red, blue and green.
I can see the mermaids swishing their shiny tails.
The tails are a different colour like red, blue and green.
I can see the seahorses, gently gliding through the underworld.
The seahorses are different colours, like red, blue, and green.

**Shannon Smith  (10)**
**Cuerden Church School**

# A Walk In The Park

A gentle, soft walk in the park
The tweeting birds' songs, as sweet as sugar
The breeze of the wind, as soft and kind as a puffy fluffy cloud
Bicycle bells ringing and pinging
Like a church bell's dong
Picnics here, there, everywhere
Crunching sounds of munching mice
But now it's time to fly.

**Jack Turner  (10)**
**Cuerden Church School**

# Fairy

Fairies twinkle in my head
Fairies twinkle in my bed
It's just like I can fly
Like a fairy in the sky
It's like I am in Neverland
The one fairy I can rely on is nice
She has fairy dust to make me
I went to Fairyland
It is very good, you should go tonight.

**Jayne Monks (10)**
**Cuerden Church School**

# Rainbows

Seven colours in the air
Spreading joy everywhere,
On the rainbow there's so much to do
When leprechauns are jumping over with you.

Red, yellow, orange, blue and white
Those five colours are so bright,
Shining brightly in the sun
Rainbows are so much fun.

At the end you will behold
A very little pot of gold,
All the gold is multicoloured
People hide gold in the cupboard.

You can hear children laughing
Fun is what people are having,
You can touch multicoloured gold
Leprechauns you can hold.

You can see a pot of tea
That a leprechaun holds for me,
You can smell the toast and waffles
The leprechaun has got the coffles.

**Dawn Ditchfield (10)**
**Cuerden Church School**

# The Lost Alien

I met an alien on the way to school
He looked really funny and sounded really cool
He said he came from planet Mars.
He said, 'That's the one'
The planet's far away, near the stars.
As he was saying his name was Ron
I said, 'What is the matter lad?'
A spaceship landed and hopped out his dad
He said, 'Thank you for helping.'
Then his spaceship started melting
We're maybe not going to planet Mars
The planet far away, near the stars.

**Amy Robertson  (9)**
**Cuerden Church School**

# The Water Lily

Something is floating down the river
And it is coming here thither,
The bottom's green, the top's pink
It could be alive, I think.

It's like a ball of bright pink flames,
The thing looks fierce, don't call it names,
The monster is sitting on a lime-green tray,
I'm now too scared to chase it away.

This thing is very deceiving,
It's trying to make me think it's leaving,
Oh no! He's coming nearer!
I think I'll run faster than Alan Shearer!

After he's eaten me, I'll be remembered by showbiz
So goodbye Mum, goodbye Auntie Liz!
Oh silly me! Why didn't I see?
It's not a monster, no, it's a water lily!

**Ann Scrivens (10)**
**Cuerden Church School**

# My Pets

My pet rabbit is so funny
My pet rabbit has a baby bunny
They both are white with a patch of grey
And at night they cuddle in the hay.

My pet dog is a golden retriever
Her favourite toy is a squeaky mouse
And she never wants to leave her
My dog likes to eat bones all day long
Then she licks the bowl with the tip of her tongue.

I also have a cat named Trixie
She likes to chase her friend the pixie
She found her at the back of our shed
Trixie has a favourite hobby, that's a thought
Yes, she likes to sleep at the end of my bed.

My pets are the best
The best you could ever find
My pets are lovely, sweet and kind
I love my pets, of course I do
My rabbit named Nibbles
My cat named Trixie
And my dog named Sue.

**Jodi Moore  (10)**
**Cuerden Church School**

# Changes

Winter is fun with all my friends
While we skate until the day ends
And then when it does we all have a smile
I smell the hot creamy teas
And hear the children laughing and giggling
In the light breeze.

Spring is fun with all my friends
While we play in the park
And splash where the stream bends.

The flowers are blooming all over the park
And the sheep and the birds are enjoying themselves
The taste of barbecues sizzling away
Oh, that really does make my day.

**Naomi Evans  (10)**
**Cuerden Church School**

# Felt-Tip Pens

I bought some felt-tip pens,
Red, yellow and blue,
I've only got three, but it will do.

I draw pictures then colour them in,
You have to colour in the lines,
So it's a good job the pen tips are fine.

At half-past two,
I put them away,
But something happened the very next day.

I couldn't find my felt-tip pens,
Red, yellow and blue,
I couldn't remember where I'd put them at half-past two.

At twelve o'clock it was dinner time and wet play,
I looked out of the window,
The sun peered through,
Then I noticed the red, yellow and blue.

The yellow and red made the sun,
The blue made the sky,
They made a lovely view
Just for me and you!

**Dani Moore (10)**
**Cuerden Church School**

# World Cup Fever

I woke up one morning
I heard a loud noise
I went to investigate
To see what it was
I jumped out of bed
My heart was beating
My teeth were chattering
What could it be?

It was fat and juicy and scary as well
Shaking and trembling
It wouldn't stand still
'Who are you?'
It replied, 'I am the ghost of England's footballers!'

**Alice Bridges  (10)**
**Cuerden Church School**

# England

England are going to score goals
With the shooting, super balls.
Brazil are going to get nil
And England get a footie drill.
They're going to do an amazing skill
With not one scoring bill.
We're playing in red
Not in my bed.
We're wearing face paints
Supporting our mates.

**Danielle Kay  (8)**
**Cuerden Church School**

# England

England are the best
Better than all the rest.
They play in white and red
Win the World Cup, they said.
Steven Gerrard is the best
England will put them to the test.
Rooney's broke his toe
He's got to go!
Gerrard, Gerrard thinks he's so hard
Then he gets a red card!

**Mellisa Allonby (9)**
**Cuerden Church School**

# England Is The Best

England are the best
Yes, you can guess.
They are the best
They can beat the rest.
This is now the time to rest
Because we are the best.
And we are going to win the test
With our hairy chests.
So we all say, 'England is the best
Better than the rest!'

**Lauren Smith  (8)**
**Cuerden Church School**

# England

Football is crazy, football is cool
Rooney's rich and England rule.
Lampard, Lampard, score that goal
Score it quick before that Paul.
Rooney's house is totally cool
I might go outside and jump in the pool.
Wave that flag high in the air
Football is all it takes to be a millionaire.
Football is crazy, football is fun
So all go home, the fun is done.

**Georgia Madden  (9)**
**Cuerden Church School**

# England

England are the winners, winners, winners.
England are the winners, winners, winners.
England are the best, watch them lift up their vests.
Rooney, Rooney broke his toe and he's got some dough.
Gerrard, Gerrard thinks he's so hard and for that he's got a red card.
England are the best, they will win above the rest.

**Natasha Kuerschner  (8)**
**Cuerden Church School**

# England

We're playing in red
But I've got to go to bed.
Walcott shoots
With his lovely new boots.
We will beat Brazil
A couple of goals to nil.
Rooney shoots
With a lovely boot.
We're all looking at the ball
But Lampard just had to fall.
Beckham shoots with a lovely free kick
But the ball got hit by sticks.
Come on England
We won't chant for Finland.

**Jack Carr (9)**
**Cuerden Church School**

# England

England are the best
Better than all the rest
Watch them score a goal
And hear a cheer from Ms Soul.
Beckham and Rooney walk onto the pitch
Ronald gets a stitch.
Gary Neville got a red card
Watch him sulk off in a nark.

**Aaron Holland (9)**
**Cuerden Church School**

# Summer

Time for the beach, waves lapping gently onto the shore.
Time for the flowers to bloom.
Time for the paddling pool.
Time for achievements going on at school.
Time for the barbecue, sizzling sausages.
Time for holidays.
The happiest time of the year.

**Callum Leithes  (8)**
**Cuerden Church School**

# Summer Is A Time For . . .

Summer is a bright new season
Summer is a time for fun
Summer is a time for leaping through the grass
When the birds are flying high.

**Ben Duckworth (8)**
**Cuerden Church School**

# Summer Is . . .

The red roses coming out with the sun
And the little bunny rabbits playing in the sun
There are some little boys and girls playing too
The girls and boys were good.

**Alex Ashworth (7)**
**Cuerden Church School**

# Summer Is . . .

A time when you can get your swimming pool out.
A time when you see the birds singing in the trees.
A time when you go to the beach.
A time when you play out for fun.
A time you have fun at school.
A dream of angels.

**Jake Holt (7)**
**Cuerden Church School**

# Summer

Summer is hot and sunny
The birds sing in summer every day
Time to go to the beach
Put up your paddling pool
Sunbathe at the beach
And out in your back garden
Play football and go on your trampoline.

**Reece Thomas  (8)**
**Cuerden Church School**

# Summer Is . . . Beautiful

A great season to have fun
I like to play with everyone.
The golden sun above the park
And even the dog who can't bark.
Animals are just like us, and all the bees
Going *buzz, buzz, buzz.*
The bright yellow sun shining over my garden
A nice cold drink, ooh, burp! Pardon.
Paddling in my pool, dancing round like a fool.
Singing all day long, singing my all time favourite song.
Butterflies zooming past all the flowers
A great day out at Alton Towers.
I like to play with all my friends
But the summer doesn't last all year, so it ends
Summer will come back soon,
Now it will end and it's only the afternoon.

**Chelsea Porter (8)**
**Cuerden Church School**

# Summer Is . . .

A time of year that is good to play.
Dolphins splash in the sparkling waves.
Ships come in every day.
People play on the beach and paddle in the sea.
Children and friends go to places where they can play.
People on ships look at all the animals in the wild sea.
Birds sing every morning to wake people up.
Children play and crash about in the summer and they play out.
People play in their paddling pools with their friends.
Animals pant for water.
Animals wake from hibernating.
Sharks feed on the bottom of the deep, shiny ocean.
People dive in the ocean and take pictures of sunken ships
and hiding animals.

**Tyler Walmsley (8)**
**Cuerden Church School**

# Summer is . . .

The golden sun burning against our faces
Ice cream melting in our mouths
The silver-blue waves hitting the shore
Birds singing softly in the trees
The clouds as soft as rabbit's fur
Water fights going on and on
The wind standing straight and stiff
Children skipping and singing merrily in the sun
The sand burning our feet
Bees buzzing from one flower to another
The dogs running and barking around the green grass
Families eating Sunday dinner
The boyfriends and girlfriends holding hands in the sun.

**Rhianna Thomas (8)**
**Cuerden Church School**

# Summer

Summer is hot
Summer is the season for a swimming pool
If I jump in the pool I'll get nice and cool
In your swimming trunks you can go to the beach and sunbathe
You can also go swimming in the sparkling sea.

**Billy Scanlon  (7)**
**Cuerden Church School**

# Summer

Summer is calm and gentle.
Birds singing sweetly in the trees.
Butterflies fluttering from flower to flower.
Trees swaying backwards and forwards, from side to side in the
gentle breeze.
Dolphins jumping in and out of the water.
Mermaids brushing their wet, silky golden hair, their tails splashing in
the water.
Lots of mermaids sit on rocks behind a waterfall.
Fish swimming through the water gracefully.
Girls skipping to school singing, boys giggling up the hill.

**Shannon Scanlon (7)**
**Cuerden Church School**

# Summer

Summer is great, summer is great
I walk through the park and I meet a mate
In the summer you get the pool out and splash about
                              and splash mums and dads
Summer is fun because you get to play good and cool fun games
Summer is great, summer is great, summer is really great
Summer is the time for the beach.

**Dominic Walmsley  (7)**
**Cuerden Church School**

# Summer

Summer is hot and sweaty, red flowers coming out of the ground.
Summer is the time for the beach, in the sun.
Summer is time for the paddling pool.
Summer is the time for insects.
Summer is the time for a water fight.

**Matthew Jones (8)**
**Cuerden Church School**

# The Criss-Cross Caterpillar

The criss-cross caterpillar
Criss-crossed an insect killer
As he criss-crossed a cedar tree
His favourite leaf for his tea
He carried on, *munch, munch, munch*
All the way through breakfast and lunch.

He creepy-crawled down the tree
Feeling full from his tea
He stopped to chat with some town folk
Sometimes cracking up a joke
But soon he settled down for bed
To rest his very sleepy head.

He wrapped himself in a cocoon
Blocking out the sun and moon
And after winter had gone by
He turned into a butterfly!

Now criss-cross caterpillar
Is not afraid of any killer
Cos he can just fly away
With no cares in his way
What a life for something so small
Isn't it such a ball!

**Emily Helm (11)**
**Garstang Community Primary School**

# Cats

*(This poem is dedicated to my three wonderful pets, Charlie, Stanley and Cat. May they rest in peace)*

Cute and fluffy were my cats
Always running across the mats
On the sofa their claws would grasp
Except at teatime, when they'd come fast
Friendly was Charlie, the black and white puss
Curious was Stanley, the one who would fuss
Cat was the one who at the end was kittenish
He always wanted dog food in his dish
I live in the house that they would share
But now they are all up in the air
Floating above in the sky
Where they will look down and say goodbye.

**William Yates (11)**
**Garstang Community Primary School**

# Space

Empty, deserted, blank, bare
Space was boring, nothing there,
Until a shooting star came flying by,
Lots of things I started to spy.

Planets, meteors, stars and rockets,
Flying high with the comets,
Swishing, whooshing through the sky
Past the sun and moon I did fly.

Crash-landed on Mars,
I could still see lots of stars,
Saw some aliens flying by,
They had six legs, goodness knows why!

I got the spaceship going again,
But it kept on going wrong, it was a pain,
I crash-landed on Earth but I'm still alive
It's quite a wonder I managed to survive.

**Anna Crowther  (10)**
**Garstang Community Primary School**

# Billy

My dog Billy
Is really silly
He likes to play all day
Especially on Jessica's birthday.

Billy is so cute
And hates to eat fruit
His fur is like silk
And he loves to drink milk.

**Amy Winder (11)**
**Garstang Community Primary School**

# Pussycats

Cats are small
Cats are sweet
Cats will snuggle up by your feet.

Cats are lovable
Cats are caring
Cats will rub against what you're wearing.

Cats are always warm and cuddly
Cats will give you lots of love
Cats are worthy of a great big hug.

My cat is called Florence
She's thirteen years old
And to me she's worth a million
Blocks of gold.

I love cats!

**Adam Baldwin (11)**
**Garstang Community Primary School**

# Fear

Fear is grey like the mist in the caves of Mount Doom.

Fear makes you feel scared like being tortured in a war camp of Hell.

Fear makes you do things like running, running away
off the face of the world.

Fear reminds you of death, like a car screeching in the night
and a boy howling in pain.

Fear is lightning like getting struck twice which blackens out your life.

**Jonathon Thompson  (11)**
**Garstang Community Primary School**

# Love

It smells sweet and flowery like blossom in the summer.
It smells like perfume wafting from a stretched pink Hummer.
It looks red and hot and all starry and stuffy.
It looks pink and beautiful, all nice and fluffy.
It makes me feel warm, like sunshine blinding on golden hay.
It makes me feel happy, like the bright sun in May.
It tastes like curry sauce, tingly, hot and spicy.
It tastes like ice cream, all creamy and icy.
It sounds like the melody of a bird.
It sounds like a heartbeat, that's what I've heard.

**Adam Stone (10)**
**Garstang Community Primary School**

# Now I've Become A Dolphin Trainer

Now I've become a dolphin trainer,
My life has turned to pure delight.
I get them ready for all their shows,
I work so hard, with all my might.

I see them gently splashing in the water,
I just love their sparkling blue and silver skin.
I hear them beautifully whistling to each other,
They wait and watch for me to jump in.

When I've got my bathing suit on,
I walk to the edge of the ocean side.
They see me diving into the water,
So off they go to swim and hide.

I dive deep down under the water,
I search in all the secret caves.
I suddenly discover a splash in the sea,
And there they are, dancing in the waves.

**Laura Sullivan  (11)**
**Garstang Community Primary School**

# Fun

Fun is yellow, like the sun shining brightly.
I feel cheerful and excited.
I taste jelly wobbling on a plate.
I want to play with all my friends.
I see the sun shining brightly in the clear blue sky.
I smell daffodils swaying in the breeze.
I hear children laughing and shouting in the playground.
I get reminded of times when I have played with my family.

**Emilie Bickerstaff  (11)**
**Garstang Community Primary School**

# My Budgie

I had a little budgie
His name was Joey Blue
And every time I talked to him
He always thought he knew
He hopped about from perch to perch
And swung from swing to swing
And every time I let him out
He would always start to sing.

**Shannon Knape (11)**
**Garstang Community Primary School**

# Storm Recipe

A storm is evil cooking up trouble
A hint of anger makes sanity crumble
A pint of explosion mixed with madness
A trace of distress causing crackles of violence.

The main big ingredient you ought to all know
Is a load of hatred making each deadly blow
But the hatred is useless without the chef
The Devil, the witch, breathing dreadful breath.

The reason it's dark, you will be told,
Is abuse and offence gone rotten in mould
And the lightning only shoots
In places with evil mutes.

**Sam Briault  (11)**
**Garstang Community Primary School**

# Fear

Fear is blue like a sea swaying in the dead of night.
Fear is silent like someone creeping up on you, not knowing
they are coming
Grey clouds dripping tears on you.
Terrified, nervous and you can sometimes feel your heartbeat.
Scream! Scream for life for hunger and for death.
Fear tastes like rice; they both leave your taste buds dry.
Fear can remind you of fright, fright creeping up in the night.
Fear smells like fish fresh for the sea, *urgh!*

**Katrina Symons  (10)**
**Garstang Community Primary School**

# The Amazing Present

It was an obscure morning,
My mother was calling,
The clock chimed nine am,
The little bird came out again.

The sky was blue,
Now I'm a year older than you,
I went to find my presents,
Instead I found a pheasant.

It had a label on its bright red neck,
It said, *To Sophie, happy birthday from Peck,*
Without realising I cried, 'Oh heck!
This present must be from Beck.'

She always gave me silly presents,
Some of them were pleasant,
But this one was quite weird,
Then Beck burst into the room and cheered,
'Happy birthday Sophie!'

**Sophie Greenwood  (11)**
**Garstang Community Primary School**

# Fear

Fear is black like a creeping panther.
Fear is silent like prey hiding from its predator.
It tastes like sour lemons.
The smell is strong, like garlic sizzling in an oily pan.
Fear is weather, grey and miserable.
Fear is being scared of something or someone near or around.
I feel scared and frightened like a cowering animal.
Fear looks like a stormy day.

**Jessica Ford  (11)**
**Garstang Community Primary School**

# Animals

Elephants are fat
Snakes are thin
Their tongues stick out
And then back in.

Whippets are thin
Cats are fat
They're thin as a pin
They're fatter than a hat.

Giraffes are tall
Mice are short
Both have got tails
But mice are small.

**James Gibbins  (11)**
**Garstang Community Primary School**

# My Dog Penny

She can sing
She can dance
She can do the disco trance.

She is hairy
She is fluffy
She is a fun packed puppy.

She is cute
She is cuddly
She is very warm and snugly.

She is cool
She is wicked
She is very good at cricket.

She is hot
She is cold
She never does what she is told.

She is funny
She is mad
She is my dog Penny
And I am very glad she is mine.

**Shane Taylor  (10)**
**Garstang Community Primary School**

# Futurama

My favourite one of the group is Bender
I adore the episode when he changes gender
I also like Leela because she's so keen
I really like the one with the *what if?* machine.

I am dead keen on Fry
'Cause he always seems to lie
Bender's always bending
His scenes seem never-ending.

Hermes Conrad is Jamaican
Yet I've seen him eating bacon
The dumbest is the professor
He's hardly a snappy dresser.

I like the one where they're collecting honey
The rich one, Amy, has always got money
Flexo's just like Bender, but with a beard
They're both the same, but Flexo's just not as weird.

**Alistair Swarbrick (10)**
**Garstang Community Primary School**

# Monkey

I like monkeys
I think they're funky
They're very cute
And like to eat fruit
They swing in trees
And pick each other's fleas.

**Jessica Preston (10)**
**Garstang Community Primary School**

# My Great Nanna

My great nanna at ninety-three
Is so very special to me.
I just love to see that cheery face
And her nightgowns are prettily dressed with lace.
Her favourite snack, Walnut Whips
And long ago, tripe and chips!
A sewing machinist was her trade
With all her clothes beautifully handmade.
Never touch her newly permed hair
But don't worry, you wouldn't dare!
She's practically perfect in every way
Just like Mary Poppins would say!

**Helen Winstanley  (11)**
**Garstang Community Primary School**

# In The Jungle

The monkey swings from tree to tree
And lands on a grizzly eating his tea on a canopy.
The elephant in the jungle tramples the way
Through the scary jungle and eats a grass bundle.
The terrifying tiger pounces at the passers-by,
As if they were an apple pie
Flesh and blood everywhere, *tear, tear, tear!*
The smell is in the air, so beware!
In the jungle the lion roars while killing his prey with his
mighty sharp paws.

**Joshua Crouch, Curtis Rogers & Lewis Bingham (11)**
**Garstang Community Primary School**

# Fear

Fear is as grey as the caves on the mountain tops
As grim as the Reaper inside that hole.
Fear is someone being shot in the head
Ripping and tearing away at your soul.

Fear is so cold it slithers up your spine
It makes me so scared, it makes me shiver.
It sounds like a werewolf howling in the night
It looks so bad and tastes like liver.

**Alex Dodd  (10)**
**Garstang Community Primary School**

# The Jungle Island

On an unknown island, in the middle of the sea
Where it was said, no human would ever be,
A monsoon had just passed,
And for the island's inhabitants, the trees were dry at last.

In the top of the green leaved canopy,
Drooling baboons scowl down at passers viciously.
But in the heart of the island is the king of the jungle
In a fortress of vines, in a jumble.

Elephants roam and wander round, searching for a water lake,
While hanging from the tropical tree branches hides the camouflaged
snake,
Then comes the kings, the lions, for their hunt
And every animal knows it could be their time and in their throats
grow a lump.

**Jack Farrar  (11)**
**Garstang Community Primary School**

# Giraffes

Giraffes are very slow and graceful
They're so friendly and delightful
They're yellow and a murky brown
They sleep standing up, they don't bend down!
They're used to the hot, fiery weather
And have skin as smooth as silky leather.

**Lauren Kemp (11)**
**Garstang Community Primary School**

# The Dream Box

*(Based on 'Magic Box' by Kit Wright)*

I will put in my box . . .
A dragon flying through the night sky,
A bird carrying a suitcase,
A fish sunbathing.

I will put in my box . . .
The smell of cheese,
The sound of noisy traffic,
A rough rock on a stormy beach.

I will put in my box . . .
A storm brewing on a dark night,
The colour blue from a rainbow,
Pizza cooking in the oven.

I will put in my box . . .
A beach empty and deserted all for me,
The feeling of soft silk,
The warmth of a fire.

My box is made of wood in the middle,
Steel around the edges and silk in the middle.
My box will go in a hidden forest.

**Yolanda Holden (10)**
**Lord Street Primary School**

# My Dream Box

*(Based on 'Magic Box' by Kit Wright)*

I will put in the box . . .
The bluest part of every ocean,
A roaring inferno, straight from the centre of the Earth,
The scent of melt-in-the-mouth dark chocolate.

I will put in the box . . .
A slight breeze going across the beach,
The deafening boom of thunder,
The leaves of palm trees as huge as cars.

I will put into the box . . .
The calmest place in the whole world,
A picture of all my family together
And the most colourful tropical fish.

My box is as fashionable as a forest
With my name engraved in gold on it
And an emerald lock with diamonds surrounding it.

I will swim in my box in the deepest part of the ocean
Then float to the top and watch the sunset.

**Jak Manser (11)**
**Lord Street Primary School**

# My Dreams Box

*(Based on 'Magic Box' by Kit Wright)*

I will put in my box . . .
The bounce of a ball racing down the street,
The taste of melting chocolate dripping down my throat,
The smell of a Chinese feast drifting up my nostrils as we drive past.

I will put in my box . . .
A rock from the beach I went to in Spain,
A pinch of the warm sand,
A warm feeling from within my heart.

I will put in my box . . .
Three roses which fill my heart with joy,
The sadness of a loved one that lingers in my mind,
The first laugh of a newborn baby.

My box is fashioned from memos and silk and steel
With hearts on the lid and whispering in the corners.
Its hinges are strong and silver.
I shall swim in my box as it is so wide,
I shall keep it in my wardrobe where a secret should be.

**Jade Phair (11)**
**Lord Street Primary School**

# My Secret Box

*(Based on 'Magic Box' by Kit Wright)*

I will put in the box . . .
The roar of a lion in the blazing heat of Africa,
The meaning of a cat standing next to an empty bowl,
The hissing of a fire on a cold winter's night.

I will put in the box . . .
A bolt of lightning as it cracks through the sky like a whip,
The fire of a barbecue trying to kick food off,
The eyes of a sly lion shimmering like diamonds.

I will put in the box . . .
The first words of a treasured baby,
The delicacy of a spider's web
And a horse that moos and a cow that neighs.

**Holly Steele-Robinson (11)**
**Lord Street Primary School**

# The Magic Box

*(Based on 'Magic Box' by Kit Wright)*

I will put in the box . . .
The sweet taste of apples,
A sizzling smell passing through the air,
A nice, red, everlasting flame of a candle.

I will put in the box . . .
An exploding volcano's roar,
My dreams of being a professional skateboarder,
A baby's first giggle appearing on the Earth.

I will put in the box . . .
A house where I'd live,
My comfy bed.

I will put in the sound of the sea crashing on the rocks.

My box was made by the iceberg which sank the Titanic,
The corners are made from gold and silver
A secret key and a lock made out of crystal.

**Jordan Brown  (10)**
**Lord Street Primary School**

# My Memory Box

*(Based on 'Magic Box' by Kit Wright)*

I will put in my box . . .
The memory of my first tooth,
The memory of my first birthday
And the memory of my brother's birth.

I'll put in my box . . .
The memory of my first summer and winter,
The memory of my first spring and autumn
And my friends and family, oh don't forget Bump.

I'll put in my box . . .
The memory of meeting Lord Street,
The memory of meeting my teachers,
And the loving memory of my boyfriend.

My box is made of silk and the hinges are felt.
The texture will be soft and silky.

When I open my box I can see all my emotions
And all of my happy and sad feelings
Are stuck in the corners.

The colours will be baby-blue, baby-pink and lilac.
I would put in all the melons and coconuts in the world,
Oh and chocolate.

It smells of cutting grass.

It sounds of a summer's day,
With the birds singing,
The crashing waves on the beach
And the laughter of children.

I would put a cold winter's day in it,
Sitting in front of the fire,
I would keep it in my secret drawer.

**Lauren Ann Goodship (11)**
**Lord Street Primary School**

# My Secrets Box

*(Based on 'Magic Box' by Kit Wright)*

I will put in my magic box . . .
The sound of waves clashing on the shore,
The swish of a silk sari on a summer night,
Photographs from when I was a baby,
My feelings about what I felt when my Uncle Bill died,
                              it was very upsetting,
Photographs of me and my sister when we were younger,
That sound of smashing windows.

I will put in my magic box . . .
The stories about my mum when she was younger,
People chatting to each other on the streets,
My memories about me and my family
And remember what I have done in life and forget all about the fears,
Secrets that my best mates have told me,
My feelings when I'm sad and feeling down in the dumps.

I will put in my magic box . . .
People whispering and shouting and yelling
When people are trying to tell each other secrets.

**Aimee Randle  (11)**
**Lord Street Primary School**

# My Feelings Box

*(Based on 'Magic Box' by Kit Wright)*

I will put in my box . . .
The colourful sunset and the whistling breeze,
The lively music going round in my head,
The ripples on the ocean and the bright tropical fish.

I will put in my box . . .
A mysterious land which has not yet been discovered,
The most difficult maths problem and the most confusing crosswords,
The sound of the floorboards creaking in the middle of the night.

I will put in my box . . .
The smell of lavender filling your nostrils,
The delightful taste of cool, fresh lemonade,
The sound of birds tweeting and the bees buzzing.

I will put in my box . . .
The memory of a loved one clinging in my head,
The sound of children crying in their room,
The unhappiness of parents arguing or shouting haunts some still.

My box is made of the strongest metal and yet it's as soft as a pillow,
With feelings on the outside and inside it opens up new secrets,
With hidden feelings in the most unusual places,
                    just to be opened one day soon.

**Sophie Regan  (11)**
**Lord Street Primary School**

# The Magic Box

*(Based on 'Magic Box' by Kit Wright)*

I will put in my box . . .
The sparkle of a star,
The smell of my grandma's rice pudding,
The smell of a candle burning.

I will put in my box . . .
The painful sting of a scorpion's tail,
The bite of a crab's pincers,
The sense of pain rushing through our body, like touching a
                                          burning flame.

I will put in my box . . .
A wish that brings back people in my family that have died,
A wish that will bring back my grandad's jokes
And the biggest smile I ever got when my grandad and grandma were
together.

**Andrew Storey (10)**
**Lord Street Primary School**

# My Magic Box
*(Based on 'Magic Box' by Kit Wright)*

I will put in my box . . .
The smell of a woman's perfume,
The hiss of a cat
And the roar of a lion.

I will put in my box . . .
The one and only George Best,
The real signed picture of Rooney
And the whole England team.

I will put in my box . . .
The best diamond in the world,
The finest day of them all
And the cutest puppy.

I will put in my box . . .
The world,
All the gadgets in the world
And all the laser guns in the world.

**Luke Ormerod  (10)**
**Lord Street Primary School**

# My Magic Box

*(Based on 'Magic Box' by Kit Wright)*

I will place in my box . . .
The dream that flew out of my hands,
The freedom of Kiais from fighting karate,
The wild scream of a blackboard.

I will put in my box . . .
The first tear from my nana,
The aroma wafting off a fresh-out-of-the-oven apple pie,
A beam from the sun.

I will place in my box . . .
The sense of an acorn crashing down onto my head,
A dog that miaows
And a cat that barks,
The howl from a ferocious lady werewolf.

In my box I will form a new sensation for a high ride roller coaster
That will finish on a glorious exotic beach.

My box looks like it was fashioned in the eighties
But inside it's full of mixed emotions and feelings,
With hinges like steel, my delicate box may not break easy,
Though inside it feels like a tender pillow, never emitting.

My box will be kept in one secret drawer with one key never to be
found.

**Harriet-Faye Webber  (11)**
**Lord Street Primary School**

# The Dream Box

*(Based on 'Magic Box' by Kit Wright)*

I will put in the box the blue ocean, breezing with love in the air.
I will put in the box the shimmer of a rainbow sparkling in the sky.
I will put in the box thoughts of myself, running with a football,
                                                    scoring a goal.
I will put in the box my dream that swished from side to side
                                            with love from my family.
Dreams can make people happy or sad and their feelings
                                            can drop down
And the loving memory of Tyler Farrow.

**Louise Townson  (11)**
**Lord Street Primary School**

# My Magic Box

*(Based on 'Magic Box' by Kit Wright)*

I will put in the box . . .
An ocean fantasy exploding before my eyes,
My silver plated chain,
Photos of dogs and my family.

I will put in the box . . .
A hot apple pie,
Lots of fish and chips,
A gorgeous fruit salad.

I will put in the box . . .
The colour of electric blue,
A nice, warm, welcoming feeling.

The box will be fashioned with lots of silver,
An electric blue lock,
Barking of dogs.

I will keep my box under my bed
Where it can bring me lots of good memories.

**Adam Cockcroft (11)**
**Lord Street Primary School**

# My Magic Box

*(Based on 'Magic Box' by Kit Wright)*

I will put in my box . . .
The venom from a tarantula,
The fire from a Japanese dragon,
The beautiful diamonds and rubies around a glorious queen.

I will put in my box . . .
A witch doing magic,
A picture of my baby cousin,
An acorn off a golden bell.

I will put in my box . . .
The roaring waves that spin,
The sound of a lion roaring for help,
The sweet and juicy smell of bacon.

I will put in my box . . .
A dragon with a roar that makes a palace crumble,
A horse's cry for help,
The rattle from a rattlesnake.

My box is fashioned with gold and silver and copper and steel,
It is closed with a dinosaur tooth,
It has gold and copper sides.

**Nathan McKenzie (11)**
**Lord Street Primary School**

# The Magic Box

*(Based on 'Magic Box' by Kit Wright)*

In my box I will put . . .
A rat being hissed at by a cat,
A candle being lit in the midnight sky,
A young face crying in the sun,
The tip of a tongue touching a tooth,
The first smile of my friend,
And an archer spreading glitter.

**Samantha Sears  (11)**
**Lord Street Primary School**

# My Secrets Box
*(Based on 'Magic Box' by Kit Wright)*

I will put in my box . . .
A beautiful picture of Stacy,
The sharp point of a diamond's edge
And the whispering of my sisters.

I will put in my box . . .
The sound of my favourite song billowing through my speakers,
A crinkled face screeching in a storm,
A devil stabbing his fork through an innocent child's heart.

I will put in my box . . .
A wild cheetah chasing after its prey,
The scent of a raspberry candle
And a hot chocolate fudge cake melting in the oven.

My box would be made of chocolate,
It would have cream and diamonds all over the hinges,
It would be made of solid gold.

I shall sleep in my box on a great, high mountain,
Then tumble down into a meadow full of chocolate.

**Billy Fryer (11)**
**Lord Street Primary School**

# My Mystery Box
*(Based on 'Magic Box' by Kit Wright)*

I will put in my box . . .
A piece of the whitest cloth,
A candle flickering, burning red flames,
A touch of the brightest millennium diamond.

I will put in my box . . .
A piece of smooth hot rock from the burning volcano,
A piece of Dairy Milk Caramel, as tasty as ice cream,
A tightrope that I couldn't cross.

I will put in my box . . .
Tutankhamen's case from my beloved uncle,
A football bouncing at top speed,
A serpent's tail full of black, cold blood.

I will put in my box . . .
A crooked lead from my favourite pencil,
A picture of my deadly enemies and my joyful friends,
A piece of my mum and dad's love.

My box is shiny but not fashionable
But it still means the world to me
And here I am back in the open.

**Curtis Davies  (10)**
**Lord Street Primary School**

# My Friend Has Been Abducted By Aliens!

My friend has been abducted by aliens,
It happened on Friday night,
We were playing football in the park
And when I turned I saw a bright light.

I dropped my football on the ground
And ran as fast as I could,
I saw the park gates far away,
Through the dark and scary wood.

When I reached the park gate,
I found I was all alone,
I knew the aliens had got her,
So I ran all the way home.

I kept the awful secret,
I didn't sleep a wink,
I dreaded Monday morning,
What would the teacher think?

At nine o'clock the school bell rang,
I walked in through the gates
And there she was, in front of me,
Playing with all our mates.

When I told her why I'd run away
And how she gave me such a fright,
She just laughed and told me,
It was only her dad with a flashlight!

**Charlotte Whittaker (11)**
**Norbreck Primary School**

# The Day Families Split Up

What can you see?
Noisy children crying on the platform,
Angry guards holding upset children,
Battered suitcases flying around the platform,
Worried mothers waving at their children.

What can you hear?
Brave fathers shouting to the children,
Giant crowds talking to all their friends,
An angry train screeching out loud,
Confused children shouting goodbye.

What can you feel?
Very sad, knowing my parents may die,
Worried in case I don't see my parents again,
Angry because I have been sent away,
Calm now, so I don't hurt myself,
The country might be safer after all.

**Robert Lee (11)**
**Norbreck Primary School**

# War

What can you hear?
Coming very close,
Bombs falling right above us,
That's what we hate most.
Rifle guns loaded, footsteps coming,
The rain is falling, sounds like constant drumming.

What can you see?
Lighting up the sky,
Bombs are falling,
Are we going to die?
Marching troops coming near,
I can see guns, although it's not clear.

Waiting and waiting,
When is the war going to end?

**Frankie Fratazzi (11)**
**Norbreck Primary School**

# Evacuation

What do you see?
Sleepy children,
Wandering away from their parents,
Loving mothers crying,
Having to leave their children,
Brave fathers,
Holding on to their children and wives,
Upset girls clinging to their dolls
And their gas masks in the boxes.

What do you hear?
Sad mothers calling to their children
Telling them not to wonder,
Steaming trains screaming
As the wheels start to move,
Angry guards shouting to the parents
To stay back from the train
Upset fathers yelling goodbye.

What can you feel?
Worried children crying
Not knowing where they are going
Sad girls and boys huddling together
Anxious teenagers holding onto
Their brothers and sisters
Scared children waving to their parents
As they vanish into the setting sun.

**Rebecca Feay (11)**
**Norbreck Primary School**

# Leaving For Safety

What can you see?
Scared children sobbing as they say goodbye,
Worried mothers waving to their loved ones,
Anxious fathers dropping the suitcases,
Loved teddies held by young children.

What can you hear?
Train funnels coughing out smoke,
Screeching whistles signalling the train is about to leave,
Shouting conductors hurrying children onto the train,
Weeping children running on board.

What can you feel?
Heavy suitcases pulling on muscles,
Wet eyes sore from crying,
Cold faces battered in the wind,
The impatient train disappears over the horizon.

**Kieran Sefton  (11)**
**Norbreck Primary School**

# Goodbye

What do you hear?
I hear parents screaming for their child,
At the train station the children are wild,
The mums and dads wave goodbye,
With a tear in their eye.

What do you see?
I see trains in crowds of smoke,
With the children having a small joke,
The little ones have to keep having fun,
To make sure they don't worry their mums.

What do you feel?
I feel my heart beating hard,
With children taking their goodbye cards,
The children leave with a fright,
They hope they can get through the night.

**Jordan Butterworth (11)**
**Norbreck Primary School**

# War

What can you see?
Crying daughters clinging on to their mothers,
Tired sons holding on to their dads,
Brave and caring parents holding their children close to them,
The train is coming towards the train stop,
Children clinging on to their teddy bears.

What can you hear?
Slamming of doors,
By the children running to their parents,
The train's whistle stopping to pick up the children,
The train instructor shouting to the children, 'All aboard!'
The parents saying, 'You will be alright.'

What can you feel?
Scared children crying on the train,
Sad parents holding their tears back,
Upset mothers seeing their children off,
People worried for their loved ones.

*The parents and children wave their last goodbye.*

**Michaela Jacobs (10)**
**Norbreck Primary School**

# War Time!

What can you hear?
Shooting bullets and growing fear,
The sight of blood drowning everyone,
Time to fight, so pick up your gun,
The planes above us, that's all we can hear,
The sound of bombs exploding on the ground,
Bullets from guns lying all around,
People screaming and fighting for their lives,
Will we make it home and see our wives?

**Gina Fratazzi (11)**
**Norbreck Primary School**

# Evacuation

What do you see?
Children crying and clinging to their parents,
Mothers crying and holding onto their little ones,
Children huddled on the edge of the platform,
Their parents crammed next to their belongings,
The train coming into the station.

What do you hear?
The train coming into the station and hooting its horn,
Children coughing because of the train steam,
Shuffling their feet on the ground,
Moaning that they don't want to go on the train,
Hearing the final whistles of the train.

What do you feel?
The children feeling lonely because they will miss their parents,
They would feel sad about missing their family,
Angry fathers and very upset mothers,
The children feel sad so they drag their suitcases.

**Miri Jones  (10)**
**Norbreck Primary School**

# The Evacuees

What can you see?
Battered baggage lying on the platform
Screaming children shouting to their parents
Other children holding on to their teddy bears
Sobbing parents clinging to their kids

What can you hear?
Rattling suitcases scraping on the hard floors
Hooting trains ready to set off
Shouting conductors getting children on the trains
Crowded carriages filling up every second

What can you feel?
Worried children all around me
Anxious toddlers holding on for dear life
Scared brothers and sisters trying to be brave
*Chug-chug*, the train and children have left!

**Rebecca Nolan (11)**
**Norbreck Primary School**

# War

What can you hear?
The sound of bursting bombs exploding in the air
The sounds of guns firing, but where? Where? Where?
The soaring of the planes, fighting fiercely in the sky,
The sound of soldiers crying in pain, why? Why? Why?

What can you feel?
It's squelchy mud underneath my feet
It reminds me of home,
Our beds made really neat,
I really need a phone!

What can you see?
I can see the bombs brightly lighting the sky
And the tanks coming closer by a mile,
I can see the thick, black smoke making everyone choke,
I can see the enemy's planes bombing our folks.

**Jennie McGill (10)**
**Norbreck Primary School**

# Evacuation

What can you see?
Battered suitcases lying around,
Patched teddies fallen on the ground,
Amongst the crowds, children are crying,
Dads are stood there sighing.

What do your hear?
Screaming and shouting all around,
Guards yelling loudly, 'Get on the train!'
As the train enters the station,
Mothers are mumbling over the situation.

What do you feel?
All children look upset,
Mothers just trying to forget,
All the troubles that happened today,
Now the children are on their way.

**Chloe Biddlestone  (11)**
**Norbreck Primary School**

# The Evacuees

What do you see?
Upset children climbing onto the train,
Caring mothers waving off their loved ones,
Brave fathers standing tall,
Waving goodbye to all their families,
Soldiers marching through the platform,
Sobbing children clinging to their teddies.

What do you hear?
Smoking trains moving forward,
Crowds talking, guards shouting,
Slamming doors, people worried,
Everyone screaming,
Wondering what's going to happen,
Sad families, rubbing their eyes,
Confused people walking around, worried and sad.

What do you feel?
Worried parents, anxious children,
Shouting and waving goodbye,
An impatient conductor blowing his whistle and shouting,
Scared children wondering where they're going,
Children clinging onto their teddies,
Shouting loved ones,
Pushing through the platform.

Not wanting to leave, saying goodbye.

**Libby Matthews (10)**
**Norbreck Primary School**

# Evacuation To The Countryside

What can you see?
Sobbing children clutching onto their teddy bears,
Miserable mothers pushing their children up the stairs,
Strong fathers telling children to stay in pairs,
Gas masks in boxes for children to wear.

What can you hear?
Rushing trains making a whistling sound,
Running children stomping on the ground,
Battered suitcases being dropped all around,
Lost children being found.

What can you feel?
Ripped seats on the train,
Getting drenched in the pouring rain,
All the soldiers feeling pain,
Every child called by their name.

**Ellie Reilly  (11)**
**Norbreck Primary School**

# Wartime

The sound of soldiers moving all around,
All the bombs making exploding sounds,
The bright bombs lighting up the dark, dangerous night,
Hitler, who made the war into a big, massive fight.

The sight of men laying everywhere,
Kind people that really care,
People sweating and fighting for their lives,
Begging for the war to stop, to see their children and wives.

I can feel the dirt all over my skin,
All the people that were fat are going to be slim,
All the troubles that have happened today,
Now have gone far away.

**Laura White  (11)**
**Norbreck Primary School**

# Evacuation And War

The sound of screams deafens me,
As the soldiers approach the trench,
I am saved by things that I can see,
I'm in a muddy pool, I'm drenched,
Soldiers wondering why they came,
While they suffer with the throbbing pain.

Over my head I can hear the planes,
Thinking about home and all the strife,
My children have gone away on the trains,
I am also sad because I am missing my wife,
I am really scared, it is not a game,
I have been stabbed once before with the enemy's knife.

**Taylor Mitchell (11)**
**Norbreck Primary School**

# Bling, Bling, King

There once was a very cool king
Who had a lot of bling
He lived in France
And liked to dance
But definitely he could not sing!

**Chris Davis (11)**
**Norbreck Primary School**

# Children Are Going, Going

What can you see?
Nervous children shivering on the platform,
Upset mothers worrying about their children,
Anxious fathers biting their nails,
Big suitcases piled up on the ground.

What can you hear?
Angry trains screaming on the tracks,
Lively guards shouting, 'All aboard!'
Crying children saying goodbye,
Screeching whistles scream over the moaning.

What can you feel?
Cold hands, freezing in the chilly wind,
Heavy suitcases weighing children down,
Angry fists swelling with fear,
The train is going to the countryside.

**Matthew Lightfoot (10)**
**Norbreck Primary School**

# My Baby Sister

What I like about Jenna is that she likes to play
And when she does play she laughs and giggles,
I love the way she cries out loud for attention.

Her cute little toes and tiny button nose
Make her look even cuter,
Jenna has lovely long eyelashes and dainty chubby cheeks,
Her lovely smile is enough to make you go, *aahh*
She dribbles a lot but she has a magical sparkle in her eye
Like my mum and I,
Some say she is like my mum,
Some say she is like my dad,
But I think that she has a bit of both.

The thing I love most about Jenna
Is that she clings onto you when you hold her,
Jenna doesn't like it when I put her down
And she doesn't like it when you are banging about,
But she loves to cuddle up close to me
Especially when I sway about,
While Jenna cuddles close to me
I listen carefully to her heartbeat
And smile as I sway with this little miracle.

**Rebecca Page (11)**
**Norbreck Primary School**

# War!

The chatter of guns, killing everyone in sight,
Then a scream makes me tingle with fright,
A sound of moaning,
Even I am now groaning,
When a shell whizzes over my head,
I think I am dead,
But no, I am alive,
I have survived.

I can see black smoke swirling in the battlefield,
Creating a mist of black, bleak, poisoned air,
Barbed wire surrounds the camp,
I am struggling to walk, I have cramp,
I walk inside a trench,
A man is being hurried in,
He is dead,
In his emergency bed.

I now fear the tiredness in my heart,
As now we have to move, I am told to carry the cart,
We walk across the bridge,
It suddenly sets alight,
People running, people screaming,
I have to run,
But one is left behind,
He is killed in the flames.

**Alex Radcliffe  (10)**
**Norbreck Primary School**

# The Day At The Station

Upset parents waving goodbye, as their children get on the train,
Annoyed guards shouting at the children on the platform,
Piled up suitcases towering over the conductors,
Crying children climbing onto the train.

Speeding train's bustling into the station,
Deep-voiced conductors shouting, 'All aboard!'
Thousands of people shouting and talking to their children,
Slamming doors, as the train leaves.

Worried, as the children don't know where they're going,
Sad, to be leaving their parents behind,
Angry, to go away from home and family,
Happy, at least they will be safe.

**Joshua Bailey  (11)**
**Norbreck Primary School**

# War

What can you hear?
I hear blasting bombs going off in the sky,
Aircraft carriers being blow sky-high,
Military units are going to war,
Gunner planes are really going to soar,
A lot of people are going to die,
Yet I will not die or take to the sky.

What can you see?
I can see the mud in the trench
And the injured sitting on a bench,
The bombs in the sky
And people going by
And this is what war is like.

What can you feel?
I can feel the mud on my feet,
But that does not mean that England is beat,
Anyone will tell you that they hate the war
And that they wish that they could be out of the door,
Lots of people falling to the floor,
Wishing that they could stop the war.

**Philip Sayers (10)**
**Norbreck Primary School**

# Goodbye!

Screaming children crying on the platform,
Courageous mothers reassuring the children,
Brave fathers standing upright,
Frustrated soldiers rushing the children.

Conductors laughing with the children
And mothers' dear cries,
The train bell screeching aloud,
The sound of suitcases being dragged.

Sad children wave goodbye,
Angry children, upset yet brave,
Cuddly teddies make us feel safe,
Mum's arms wrapped around.

*Goodbye my dear children.*

**Rebekka Foy  (11)**
**Norbreck Primary School**

# The Evacuees

Platforms can make the babies cry,
Platforms, platforms, see the children crying their eyes out
Waiting for someone to take them home
Making the children laugh
Getting scared and even more scared.

Getting an upset feeling
And a lump in my throat
Clinging on to Mum, not letting go
And then kicking their legs.

Trying to get away and back home
I want to go please
Let me go home
I'll live in a cupboard
Please, I will beg you Mum
Please don't let me go.

**Kelly Hammersley (11)**
**Norbreck Primary School**

# The Evacuees

People screaming because they don't like being evacuees,
Babies crying, clinging to their mothers' knees,
The train pulls up to the platform, vibrating,
I wish it would stop so I could go back to my street,
I hear the steam hissing like a kettle,
The rhythm on the tracks sounds like my heart beating faster,
I hear babies crying because they are going to miss their mums,
The whistle blows,
The time is up,
It's time to say goodbye.

**Ashley Crooper Calland  (11)**
**Norbreck Primary School**

# Imagine

Imagine a giraffe,
Having a very loud laugh,
Imagine a frog,
Kissing a dog,
Imagine a snake,
Eating a birthday cake,
Imagine a monkey,
Being funky,
Imagine a goat,
Wearing a coat,
Imagine a snail,
With a nail,
Imagine a gazelle,
That fell into a well,
Imagine a slug,
With a pet bug,
What an amazing world it would be!

**Lauren Atha (7)**
**Roseacre CP School**

# Weekdays

Monday, can't wake up
School day, come on, let's get up
Oh no! spelling test.

Tuesday, got DT
We're making fairgrounds you see
Round and round it goes.

Wednesday, got PE
Then double literacy
We are writing poems.

Thursday, double art
ICT what a fun start
Searching for good facts.

Friday, best weekday
Not got school the next morning
End of day - best part!

**Laura Anthony (11)**
**Roseacre CP School**

# Under The Sea

Under the sea
Where we, the creatures, live
Me and my friends get up to mischief.

What do we do? You ask,
We play all day, every day,
Tickle my dad, with my eight great, long legs.

I also go to Sea Hook School,
I play all day in the big swimming pool,
Dad says I'm gifted, I never run out of fuel!

Under the sea,
Where we, the creatures live,
We all have *fun!*

**Gabriella Ann Maud Berry (11)**
**Roseacre CP School**

# Imagine

Imagine a mouse,
Living in a very small house,
Imagine a gazelle,
Putting on some gel,
Imagine a lion,
Buying an iron,
Imagine a fish,
Eating a dish,
Imagine a pig,
Going outside to dig,
Imagine a dog,
Meeting a frog,
Imagine some ants,
Wearing spotty pants,
What a strange world this would be!

**Laura Coleman  (7)**
**Roseacre CP School**

# Rainbow - Haikus

Colour of anger
Also the colour of blood
That is very bright

The colour of fire
Like the sun has exploded
Laura's hair at dawn

Shining, sparkling
Like a burning banana
Glowing like the sun

The garden colour
Outstanding grass in the sun
Beautiful hot grass

The colour of plums
Like our colourful maths books
And our felt-tip pens

Colour of petals
So very bright and cheerful
Bees love the colour!

**Alice Croft (11)**
**Roseacre CP School**

# Animals

Black stripes on orange
Long sharp claws to catch its prey
Do you know what I am?
*Tiger!*

My long, thin neck
I eat leaves from the top of trees
Do you know what I am?
*Giraffe!*

I swing from tree to tree
And I hang upside down eating
Do you know what I am?
*Monkey!*

**Shannon Cuthbert  (10)**
**Roseacre CP School**

# Mountains

Ben Nevis, the best
High to climb in the UK
Windy and cold.

All mountains are windy
Cold and wet and snowy
Or hot and sandy.

Everest in Nepal
Himalayas snowy and cold
Death summoned to fate.

Doesn't matter what size
Doesn't matter what shape
They are all mountains.

Beacon Fell, steep
Hot in summer and sunny
Good in any weather.

Mountains are great
For the challenge to climb them
In any weather.

**Christopher Dix  (11)**
**Roseacre CP School**

# The Growing Giant

You may be small, but one day you'll be tall,
Like me, maybe taller,
You won't fit into your bed, your hat won't fit on your head,
Your feet with fill up the floor,
You'll have to bend down to come through the door,
You'll be able to reach the highest shelf,
I can't do that now myself.

Out in the country the tallest trees,
Will scratch your ankles and tickles your knees,
Up in the clouds, yes, way up there,
The eagles will nest in your craggy hair,
They had better soon find a safer place,
Because soon, your head will be up in space!

**Donald Hakandu  (11)**
**Roseacre CP School**

# The Sea

He is like a hungry fox
Gnawing at the rocks
So determined to catch
Washing waves on the sandy bay
He is giant and grey
So swift, so deadly
He could eat you alive
So protective of his prey
He creeps up
Because he is green with envy
But also so calm
So silent, but so quick
But on the quiet days
In May and June
On the hill of green grass
On the sandy dunes
That's where I lay
When I'm feeling blue.

**Reece Hendry  (11)**
**Roseacre CP School**

# My School Week - Haikus

School week has started
The third lesson is music
We learn how to play.

Tuesday is English
We have double, it is fun
We do poetry.

Wednesday is so fab!
Middle of the week today
And it is DT.

It is library
Changing our library books
A great collection.

End of week today
World War II in history
ICT as well.

**Hope Hollis  (10)**
**Roseacre CP School**

# The Nightmare

I was in bed, I saw a head
And red eyes were staring at me.
My feet were tickling, prickling
I was jumping and bumping.
I was shouting and panting,
Then the bed covers came over me
And it was a *dream!*

**Bethany Hunt  (10)**
Roseacre CP School

# Seasons

Hot weather all day
People swimming in the sea
Rub their suncream in

Kids covered in leaves
Leaves are falling on people
Leaves dropping on us

A sign of new life
New eggs cracking all day
Plants growing, like us

Snowy and rainy
Wintry and very cold
The cold is so dull.

**Alexandra Isaac (10)**
**Roseacre CP School**

# Jamaica

J ammin' like Bob Marley
A ir is filled with reggae
M usic is loud and rhythmic
A mountain full of fun
I wish I was there again
C oconut trees, cool and big
A musements for everyone!

**Nathan Jackson  (11)**
**Roseacre CP School**

# Seasons

The bitter ice-cold
White flakes falling to the ground
Search for your blue scarf

New flowers blooming
Cute rabbits come out to play
Easter is coming

Go to the seaside
Play with your friends
This weather won't last

Leaves fall off the trees
Play on the ground with the leaves
Hallowe'en is here.

**Amanda Johnson  (11)**
**Roseacre CP School**

# The Perfect Shot

Haven't played since they bought me,
I really want to play,
I need to kick that football
And score the winning goal!

Cos I'm as good as the others,
They know that when they watch,
They see me score past the number one,
What a perfect shot!

**Jack Lavelle  (11)**
**Roseacre CP School**

# Hallowe'en

This is Hallowe'en
This is Hallowe'en
Red, black and slimy green

Everyone dressed
As ghosts and ghouls
All think it's really cool

All the children eating sweets
Chocolate cakes
And other treats

Lots of families
Spending money on candy
When all the parents want
Is a little drop of brandy!

Devils dressed in black and red
Real things that look
Totally dead

All the witches with pointy hats
Carrying broomsticks
And pitch-black cats

The kids knock
And get quite a scare
Mrs Kibbles in her underwear!

You never know what
You're going to see
On the night
Of Hallowe'en!

**Jordan Jessica McLellan (10)**
**Roseacre CP School**

# When I Got My First Football

When I got my first football,
I didn't know what to do,
I was in the yard,
I kicked it so hard,
I knew!
It was the kick of my dreams!

**Sam McCloy  (11)**
**Roseacre CP School**

# Bloomfield Road

B is for Bloomfield Road
L is for Liam saving a penalty
O is for 'Oh, what a cool goal'
O is for 'Oh no, it's 2-2'
M is for Mum, coming to watch me
F is for a field that I played on
I is for an impossible kick
E is for everyone on their side
L is for leaving with a cup and medal
D is for doing our best!

**Jordan Payne (11)**
**Roseacre CP School**

# Rainbow - Haikus

The scary anger
The beautiful, bright, hot sun
Colourful red, yes!

Burning orange fire
Bright sun in a clear blue sky
Laura's hair at dawn.

Sparkling colour
Like a lot of bright daisies
In the summer sun.

My beautiful top
The colour of grass and leaves
Beautiful nature.

The bright, waving sea
The pale blue sky above us
Like running water.

Indigo, dark blue
It is like a dark blue sky
Oh no, do not rain!

Violet like sunset
Beautiful flowers, oh yes
I love the sunset!

**Jasmine-Lea Senior (10)**
**Roseacre CP School**

# Imagine

Imagine a giraffe,
Having a bath,
Imagine a fish,
Washing a dish,
Imagine a parrot,
Was eating a carrot,
Imagine a shark,
Was playing in the park,
Imagine a mouse,
Who lived in a little house,
Imagine a snake,
Who was across the lake,
What a strange world this would be!

**Shashin Sood  (7)**
**Roseacre CP School**

# England's Joy - Haikus

The World Cup is back
It's coming back to England
The fans will make sure

Cheering the team on
Chanting all the chants out loud
The fans will make sure

Just like '66
We'll win it again this year
The fans won't give up

Beckham, Lampard, Cole
They will be unstoppable
The fans will enjoy

Two thousand and two
We went out in the quarters
Seaman's strange mistake

In nineteen-ninety
Misery in the semis
Gazza's sending off

Two thousand and six
This will be our finest year
Come on you England!

Walcott, seventeen
A dream coming true for him
He'll score cracking goals

And I believe that
Beckham will lift the World Cup
With pride and passion

We'll celebrate now
We'll fight to the end
The fans will make sure.

**Henry Woodsford  (11)**
**Roseacre CP School**

# Dragon

Dragon, dragon, be my friend
Dragon, dragon, don't go away
Dragon, dragon, don't be bad
Dragon, dragon, tell me a story
Dragon, dragon, don't be frightened
Dragon, dragon, I love you
Dragon, dragon, where's your family?

**Leon Baker (7)**
**St Hugh's CE Primary School, Oldham**

# The Snake That Ate The Steak

I had a snake
That ate a steak
And was more full
Than a bull
It went to sleep
As fast as me.

**Chelsea Dawson (9)**
**St Hugh's CE Primary School, Oldham**

# I Can't Breathe

I can't breathe when I run
I can't breathe in smoke
And animals bother me
I've got asthma you see

I can't breathe when I have a cold
I can't breathe when I have a bug
Being ill bothers me
I've got asthma you see

I go to a club called Bronchial Boogie
It's good
They teach me how to keep well
With lots of kids like me
Who have asthma you see

I learnt my triggers
I learnt to use my inhalers
Nothing bothers me
I've got asthma you see.

**Georgia Maltby (9)**
**St Hugh's CE Primary School, Oldham**

# When I Was A Bully

When I was a bully
I bit
I hit
I called them twits
I made them bleed
So they were in need
I made them cry
Never be a bully!

**Alex Lamb (11)**
**St Hugh's CE Primary School, Oldham**

# A Poem

The sun is red
The car is white
Everything
Turns out so bright.

**Rosie Sutton (8)**
**St Hugh's CE Primary School, Oldham**

# Summer

Summer is red and green
It tastes like cold lollipops and ice cream
It sounds like birds singing
It looks like the sun and the blue sky
It smells like daffodils I'd say
It makes me hot and happy.

**Shurayh Shuaib (8)**
**St James' CE Primary School, Haslingden**

# Autumn

Autumn is dark and yellow and red
It tastes like hot coffee and chocolate
It sounds like leaves falling and trees waving
It looks like a nice, lovely day
It smells like hot chocolate buns burning
It makes me feel very happy.

**Hafsah Begum  (8)**
**St James' CE Primary School, Haslingden**

# Monday's Child Is Scruffy And Smelly

Monday's child is scruffy and smelly,
Tuesday's child keeps on watching the telly,
Wednesday's child doesn't wash his hands,
Thursday's child couldn't just stand,
Friday's child kisses his mummy,
Saturday's child has a big, fat tummy
And the child that is born on the seventh day
Is very annoying, OK!

**Ruksana Akter (8)**
**St James' CE Primary School, Haslingden**

# Summer

Summer is yellow, white and red
It tastes like strawberries and cold water
It sounds like birds singing
It looks like sky-blue flowers
It smells like freshly-cut grass
It makes me feel hot and red.

**Fahmedah Ridwana  (8)**
St James' CE Primary School, Haslingden

# Summer

Summer is hot
It tastes like hot chilli and ice cream
It sounds like fire and seagulls
It looks like sunshine and BBQs
And it's time to go to the beach
It smells like flowers and hot dogs and burgers
It makes me feel sweaty.

**Darius Barton  (7)**
**St James' CE Primary School, Haslingden**

# Winter

Winter is icy and freezing snow
Winter is nippy and bitter
Winter is shivery, icy and cold
It tastes like warm tea
It tastes like chocolate chips
It tastes like hot bread
It sounds like a robin flying
It sounds like birds singing
It looks like snowmen and Christmas trees
It looks like snow melting
It smells warm
It makes me feel happy
It makes me feel excited.

**Thahmid Hoque  (8)**
**St James' CE Primary School, Haslingden**

# Winter

Winter is white and blue
It tastes like hot chocolate and buttered toast
It sounds like kettles boiling
It looks like snow falling
It smells like hot Ready Brek
It makes me feel cold.

**Tyler Jacques (8)**
**St James' CE Primary School, Haslingden**

# The Iron Man

T he
H uge
E normous

I ntelligent
R especting
O verjoyed
N ormal

M an is
A dventurous and
N ice.

**Hayley Morley  (11)**
**St James' CE Primary School, Haslingden**

# The Iron Man

T he
H uge
E normous

I ncredible
R obotic
O ther
N ormal

M onstrous
A ngry and
N ine feet tall.

**Naomi Mandeena (11)**
**St James' CE Primary School, Haslingden**

# The Iron Man

T he
H eroic
E arth giant

I ntellectual
R obot
O rderly
N ice

M ild-mannered
A dmired
N itwit.

**Jordan Jacques  (10)**
**St James' CE Primary School, Haslingden**

# The Iron Man

T he
H uge
E normous

I ron
R usty
O riginal
N osy

M enacing
A nd
N egative man.

**Kerry Anne Mason (11)**
**St James' CE Primary School, Haslingden**

# The Iron Man

T he
H uge
E xcited

I ncredible
R ecent
O ld
N ormal

M onster
A dventurous
N on-stop.

**Maariyah Shafiq  (11)**
**St James' CE Primary School, Haslingden**

# The Iron Man

T he
H ilarious
E normous

I ntelligent
R avenous
O utstanding
N erve-wracking

M annered
A dorable
N eat.

**Reema Rahman (11)**
St James' CE Primary School, Haslingden

# The Iron Man

T he
H uge
E normous

I nsane
R usty
O ld
N asty

M an is
A legendary
N uisance.

**Shahrakh Khan  (11)**
**St James' CE Primary School, Haslingden**

# The Iron Man

T he
H uge
E normous

I ron man
R evolving
O rdering
N aturistic book

M ight be
A bout
N ine feet tall.

**Tayyib Mohammad  (11)**
**St James' CE Primary School, Haslingden**

# The Iron Man

T all
H umorous
E xciting

I nteresting
R evolutionary
O ctagonal faced
N o hair

M an
A bout
N ine feet tall.

**Thahed Ahmed  (11)**
**St James' CE Primary School, Haslingden**

# The Iron Man

T he
H uge
E normous

I ron
R usty
O riginal
N osy

M an made from iron
A nd who is
N ameless.

**Abdullah Mohammed  (11)**
**St James' CE Primary School, Haslingden**

# The Juvenile Robin

My desk's in the middle of the room
And nobody knows
I'm a juvenile robin from a robin's nest
With down that's electric
And my beak's very sharp
As well as my claws
I have two feet and eyes
I can fire ice beams from my beak
And cut them with my claws
The children would be terrified if they knew
But nobody, nobody knows.

**Julian Shield  (8)**
**Westholme Boys' School**

# The Volvitor

I'm a volvitor
Nobody knows
Here, people think I'm just a boy
I'm as big as 100,000 elephants
My teeth are as big as a whale's
I've got thorns in my head
I've got 1500 toes
Nobody, nobody knows
I've got 200 eyes
All over my body
I can put a forcefield around myself
I can shoot the thorns out of my head
I can smash a window without touching it
I can break 16 walls
I can shoot tomatoes out of my nose
I can fly too
Wouldn't they shriek if they saw my face?
Wouldn't they squeal if they saw my body?
Will they jump out of the window like rabbits?
Nobody knows.

**George Kenyon (8)**
**Westholme Boys' School**

# The Invasion Of The Pigiwaterbottle

I am a big Pigiwaterbottle from Mars
And I keep eating chocolate bars
I sit at the back of the class
People would fear me
If they knew I had two snouts
I am a pink, red and yellow colour
I can fly and breathe ice
*I am a powerful Pigiwaterbottle!*
And I can shape-shift into anything
I can breathe in water
People would scream if they knew
That I am a Pigiwaterbottle!

**Ben Shaw (8)**
**Westholme Boys' School**

# The Pigglehogglesaurus

My desk's at the back of the class
And only I know
I'm a Pigglehogglesaurus
And I live on Pluto
My heads are green
All three of them
My belly is green
All my eyes are red
I have fifteen
Seven on each side
But I bet they would yell
At my special middle eye
They would be terrified if they knew
That my eye fired lasers too
I could blow them all up
With my lasers
And nobody, nobody knows!

**Daniel Anderson  (8)**
**Westholme Boys' School**

# The Strange Ox

I am in a café disguised as a man
I am having a nice meal from my van
But nobody, but nobody knows
I am a Strange Ox
And I come from Planet Nox
I might look strange
I might look weird
But my best friend's called Zeird
I look like a 1000 horned ox
And I like fox
If I revealed my true form
Everyone would hide and run
But did I tell you?
I am called Norm
I can fire lasers out of my 50 fingers
I will distract some singers
My colours are green, blue, red, pink and purple
My favourite song is called Snurple
I have 95 toes
And have one nose
I also have 6000 teeth
Which help me scare a thief
I can change into anything
Which makes me kick
I am 1000 metres tall.

**Alexander Poulson  (8)**
**Westholme Boys' School**

# The Shining Dull Beach

On the beautiful beach shining with light
I saw four people flying a kite
People dancing, shouting with glee
All wanting to play with me
Gleaming beach ball, we loved to play
So many games to enjoy today
Diving around on the steaming sand
Water cooling the glittering land
The sun is shining like a laser down
On the scorched, desert-like town
Teatime approaching very fast
People taking sails from the mast
The time of fun isn't over today
Tomorrow we will be back to play.

Wind coming down, sweeping the beach clean
Soaked-in thunder clouds look mean
All grey and black, the evil sky
Sand scattering, flying by -
Freezing cold, the forsaken beach
Clustered clouds, lightning for each
Sea overthrown with rushing waves
Splashing inside the rocky caves
I'm scared, frightened on this deserted shore
I'd hate to stay here anymore
I'll want to go back when it's shining bright
I'll feel fantastic in the beaming light!

**David Lee  (10)**
**Westholme Boys' School**